Fact Finders®

Awesome ENGINEERING

TUNNELS

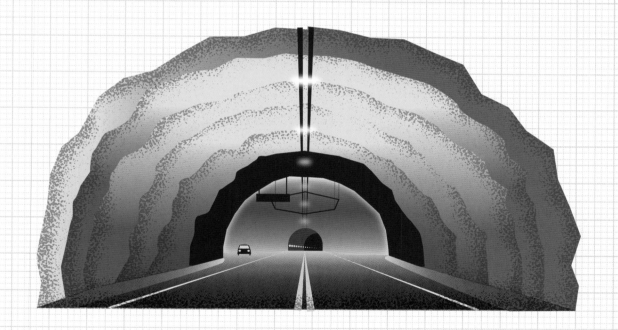

SALLY SPRAY
WITH ARTWORK BY MARK RUFFLE

CAPSTONE PRESS
a capstone imprint

Fact Finders Books are published by Capstone Press,
1710 Roe Crest Drive, North Mankato, Minnesota 56003
www.mycapstone.com

Library of Congress Cataloging-in-Publication Data
Library of Congress Cataloging-in-Publication data is available on the Library of Congress website.

978-1-5435-1338-7 (library binding)
978-1-5435-1344-8 (paperback)

Editorial Credits

Series editor: Paul Rockett
Series design and illustration: Mark Ruffle
www.rufflebrothers.com
Consultant:
Andrew Woodward BEng (Hons) CEng MICE FCIArb

Photo Credits

Aniza/Dreamstime: 28cl. Azat1976/Shutterstock: 23b. Goran Cakmazovic/Shutterstock: 8b. ESB Professional/Shutterstock: 18t. estherspoon/Shutterstock: 28r. Everett Historical/Shutterstock: 11t. Julien Hautcoeur/Shutterstock: 13b. Philip Lange/Shutterstock: 20t. Jianhua Liang/Dreamstime: 29tc. Mandritoiu/Dreamstime: 5. Mikhail Markovskiy/Shutterstock: 29tr. Shaiful Zamri Masri/Dreamstime: 28c. George Rinhart/Corbis Historical/Getty Images: 6. TonyV3112/Shutterstock: 26. Konstantin Tronin/Shutterstock: 25cr. Thor Jorgen Udvang/Shutterstock: 29tl. Tao Chuen Yeh/AFP/Getty Images: 18b.

First published in Great Britain in 2017
by The Watts Publishing Group
Copyright © The Watts Publishing Group, 2017

TABLE OF CONTENTS

CAN YOU DIG IT?

Tunnels are dug into the **landscape**, linking places and people through difficult **terrain** or even under water.

Tunnel building began around 3,000 years ago as people found ways of building safe underground links. Since then, thanks to **innovative engineering**, tunnels have become longer, deeper, and more impressive.

2180–2160 BC

Brick-lined tunnels in Ancient Babylonia (present-day Iraq) were used to move water from place to place.

36 BC

A tunnel was built connecting Naples to Pozzuoli in Italy. It featured basic **ventilation** so people didn't run out of air while underground.

1681

The Midi Canal system in France is built with a tunnel for boats. It was the first tunnel built using gunpowder to blast through rocks.

1825

Marc Isambard Brunel's invention of the tunneling shield allowed him to dig the first tunnel under a major river. This was the Thames Tunnel in London, England.

1867

In Sweden, Alfred Nobel invented dynamite to help blast through rocks.

1874

Peter M. Barlow and James Henry Greathead combined their design ideas to make a circular tunneling shield. It was used to build the world's first underground railway—the London Underground.

4

WORLD'S LONGEST TUNNELS

The world's longest tunnels supply water to towns and cities. Here are the top six:

Delaware Aqueduct, New York City: 85 mi
Päijänne Water Tunnel, Finland: 74.5 mi
Dahuofang Water Tunnel, Liaoning Province, China: 53 mi
Orange-Fish River Tunnel, South Africa: 51.4 mi
Bolmen Water Tunnel, Sweden: 51 mi
Tunnel Emisor Oriente, Mexico: 38.5 mi

Follow the tunnel to find its location.

1907

Carl Akeley invented **shotcrete**, which is **concrete** blasted onto tunnel walls using **compressed air**. This removes water, which speeds drying, but most importantly it allows concrete to be placed without the use of molds. It was first used in Chicago, Illinois.

1927

The Holland Tunnel in New York City was the first to use mechanized fans to replace the air in the tunnel.

1952

James S. Robbins invented the tunnel boring machine (TBM). This amazing machine revolutionized tunnel building.

5

THAMES TUNNEL

Built between 1825 and 1843, the Thames Tunnel was a truly revolutionary construction. The first tunnel to go below a major river, it was built using some brand-new engineering techniques. When it opened, it was known as the eighth wonder of the world.

Build a tunnel between Rotherhithe and Wapping, under the busy River Thames to allow the transport of people and goods by wagon or carriage.

Engineers: Marc Isambard Brunel, Thomas Cochrane, and Isambard Kingdom Brunel

Location: Rotherhithe to Wapping, London, England

The finished tunnel is 1,332 feet long, 36 ft wide, 23 ft high, and runs 75 ft below the surface of the water.

ENTRANCE TOWER

Marc Brunel had a clever plan for how to get underground to begin tunneling under the Thames. A 39-foot-tall circular brick wall was built on the soft ground near the riverbank in Rotherhithe. The wall was strengthened at the top and bottom with **iron** rings connected by iron rods. Soil was gently removed from under the base, and then **gravity** took over and the whole structure sank into the soil.

After two months, the top of the wall had sunk to ground level. **Foundations** were then added and part of the circular wall was removed so that tunneling could begin.

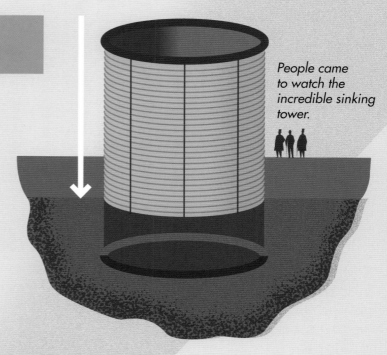

People came to watch the incredible sinking tower.

TUNNELING SHIELD

Marc Brunel and Thomas Cochrane designed the tunneling shield, which allowed many workmen to dig the tunnel at the same time.

The large rectangular frame was tall and strong enough to support the roof and sides of the tunnel while it was being built. There were three sections that men could work in, using shovels to dig out the soil. The men behind the shield laid bricks for the tunnel's walls.

The project ran out of money and the ramps for horse-drawn carriages were never built. Instead, the tunnel opened for people to walk through. By the end of 1869, it had been adapted for trains and is still used today by busy London commuters.

River Thames

To raise funds for the tunnel, it was turned into a tourist attraction with people paying to see it being built. Big mirrors were put up at the end to make it look longer than it actually was.

NEW YORK CITY SUBWAY

One of the world's largest and busiest underground rail links is the New York City Subway. It has a vast 660 mile network of tunnels, and transports nearly six million people around the city every weekday. It first opened in 1904 and has been expanding ever since.

Bronx

Harlem River →

BUILDING BRIEF

Build a rail system for a growing city to provide commuter links that won't disturb the city streets.

Engineer: William Barclay Parsons

Location: New York City, USA

Hudson River

Manhattan

Central Park

CUT AND COVER

The subway's early tunnels were built using the cut and cover method. This means that huge **trenches** were dug straight down into the streets. Wooden frames were used to support the ground, allowing the brick tunnel to be built. Once the tunnel was built, it was then covered with soil. Digging like this was difficult. Traffic was disrupted and **sewer**, gas, and water pipes had to be relocated as construction progressed.

*Wooden frames supported the **excavation** while the tunnel was built inside. Street traffic was redirected around the trenches on steel and wooden bridges.*

Wooden frame   Soil covering

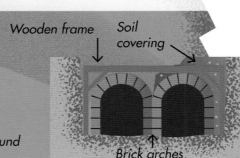

Brick arches

Tunnels were finished inside with brick arches. Concrete and steel bases were laid on the ground for the rails to be placed on.

8

HARLEM TUNNEL

One of the subway tunnels runs under the Harlem River. When work began in 1913, a trench was dug in the riverbed. **Cast iron** sections were bolted together to form the four tubes of the tunnel. The tubes were floated out to the river and sunk into the trench by filling them with water. They were surrounded and encased in concrete to keep them in place and stop them from floating away when the water was pumped out of them.

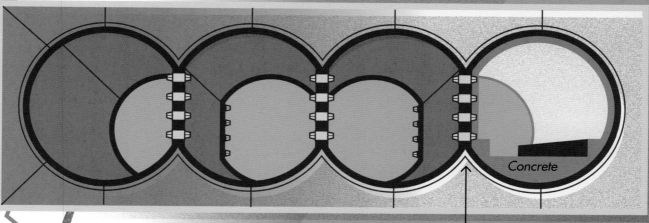

Concrete

Precast *steel bolted together*

LATER . . .

The New York City Subway has continued to grow and expand over the years to keep up with growing demand. The latest development is the 2nd Avenue Expansion, which extended tracks from Manhattan to the east side of the city. Over time, tunneling techniques have improved, so the digging work goes on right under the streets and subway lines. The workers use massive tunnel boring machines that cut through the rock without anyone above noticing.

Brooklyn

HOLLAND TUNNEL

In the 1920s, road traffic was increasing at an astonishing rate in New York City. The solution was the Holland Tunnel. Built under the Hudson River, it linked Manhattan and New Jersey and created a new road link to ease traffic jams in the busy city.

BUILDING BRIEF

Build a tunnel for busy New Yorkers to drive the ever-increasing number of motor cars in the city across the Hudson River.

Engineer: Clifford Holland and Milton Harvey Freeman, who both died during the project. It was finished by Ole Singstad.

Location: New York City, USA

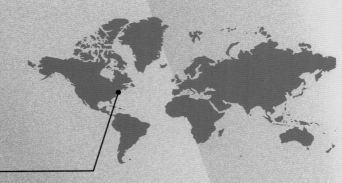

WHY BUILD A TUNNEL?

During the 1920s, ships with tall masts still sailed up the Hudson River. This meant that any bridge across the water would need to be very high to allow them to travel underneath. But in order to allow traffic to travel on and off, high bridges need a lot of space on either end—and in this case, there wasn't enough room. So a tunnel was thought to be the best solution!

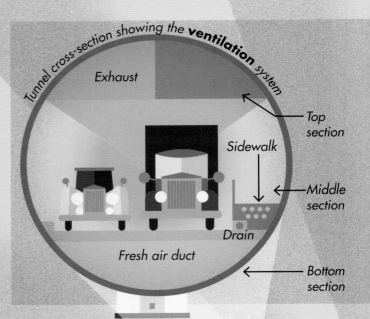

Tunnel cross-section showing the **ventilation** system

Exhaust

Top section

Sidewalk

Middle section

Drain

Bottom section

Fresh air duct

Land ventilation station

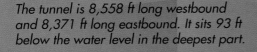

The tunnel is 8,558 ft long westbound and 8,371 ft long eastbound. It sits 93 ft below the water level in the deepest part.

CONSTRUCTION

The twin-tunnel design carries two lanes of traffic going each way. The tunnels had to be dug into the seabed by hand with the men working in **caissons**—watertight chambers made for digging under rivers. Forty-five men at a time worked in the cramped conditions, digging and blasting their way through the rock on the riverbed. The areas dug out were lined with 70,000 cast-iron supports. To finish the inside walls, 6 million **ceramic** tiles were laid.

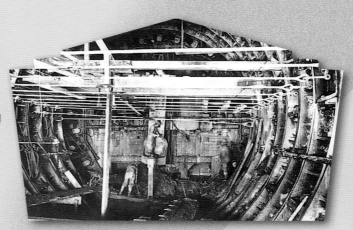

Building the tunnel in 1923

VENTILATION SYSTEM

The tunnel crossing used a revolutionary ventilation system designed by engineer Ole Singstad. He concluded that the round tunnel needed to be divided into three sections. The clean air was blown in through the bottom section, the middle section was where the roadway was laid and the upper section removed the dirty exhaust fumes. There are a total of 84 fans—42 blow clean air into the tunnels and the other 42 remove the fumes.

Air enters and exits the tunnels though four ventilation stations positioned along the length of the tunnel. Two are in the river, and the other two are on the riverbanks. The air in the tunnel is changed completely every 90 seconds. It's thought that the air in the tunnel may be cleaner than on some streets in New York City.

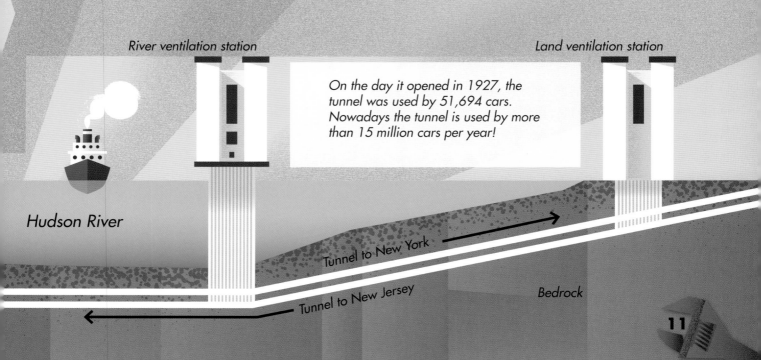

River ventilation station

Land ventilation station

On the day it opened in 1927, the tunnel was used by 51,694 cars. Nowadays the tunnel is used by more than 15 million cars per year!

Hudson River

Tunnel to New York

Tunnel to New Jersey

Bedrock

SEIKAN TUNNEL

At 33.4 mi, the Seikan Tunnel is the second-longest rail tunnel in the world. Opened in 1988, the tunnel sits 459 ft below the seabed and 787 ft below sea level. It was built to replace a dangerous ferry crossing connecting the Japanese islands of Honshu and Hokkaido.

BUILDING BRIEF

Construct a safe route between two of Japan's islands for a growing number of passengers and increase the movement of trade goods.

Engineer: Japan Railway Construction Corporation

Location: Honshu to Hokkaido, Tsugaru Strait, Japan

DIGGING DOWN

The digging of the tunnel began from both ends. The rock under the seabed would sometimes crack, so driving the tunnels forward was done by drilling through soft rock and blasting harder rock with dynamite. Dug out rubble was removed back through the tunnel by rail. Steel supports were added to the inside of the tunnel to help keep it up, with concrete sprayed over the top to form the inside lining.

HONSHU

The tunnel connects the world's first undersea railway stations: Tappi-Kaitei on Honshu and Yoshioka-Kaitei on Hokkaido.

Tappi-Kaitei Station

In 1983 the tunnels met in the middle with a final blasting of dynamite.

Pilot tunnel—now used as a → *collection area for water*

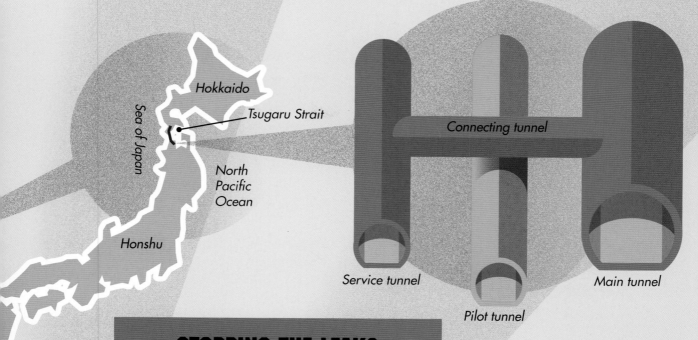

Hokkaido

Sea of Japan

Tsugaru Strait

North Pacific Ocean

Honshu

Connecting tunnel

Service tunnel

Pilot tunnel

Main tunnel

STOPPING THE LEAKS

When digging progressed below the surface of the sea, water began to leak into the tunnel, starting a constant battle to keep the inside dry. In 1976, a section of the tunnel almost a mile long flooded, and it took five months to get the flood under control. After that, engineers developed a way to **stabilize** the rock—holes were **bored** in a fan shape into the next section of rock to be dug. **Grout** was pumped into the holes to reinforce the next section to be dug out. This also helped to fill cracks in the rocky seabed where water could come in.

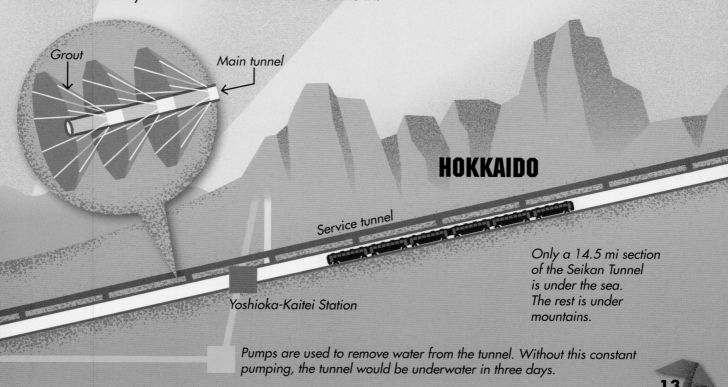

Grout

Main tunnel

HOKKAIDO

Service tunnel

Yoshioka-Kaitei Station

Only a 14.5 mi section of the Seikan Tunnel is under the sea. The rest is under mountains.

Pumps are used to remove water from the tunnel. Without this constant pumping, the tunnel would be underwater in three days.

CHANNEL TUNNEL

At more than 31 mi long, the Channel Tunnel is an engineering wonder. Not only does it have the longest undersea section of tunnel in the world (23.5 mi), but it links two different countries: England and France. The idea to build a cross-channel tunnel had been around for more than 200 years, but it didn't happen until 1988. It took around 13,000 workers six years to build it.

BUILDING BRIEF

Build a tunnel under the English Channel at the shortest point between the England and France, making a fast rail journey from London to Paris possible.

Engineering and construction:
Balfour Beatty Construction Company

Location: Folkestone, England and Coquelles, France

TUNNEL BORING MACHINES

Early studies of the ground under the English Channel found a layer of chalk marl, a type of rock that is easy for tunnel boring machines (TBM) to tackle. This layer of rock decided the route to be followed.

Behind the cutter, rock and rubble was swept onto a **conveyor belt** that loaded the material onto railcars to be taken away. But TBMs do more than just nibble through the rock—they drill holes in the tunnel surface and inject grout and bolts ready to add precast supports made of concrete.

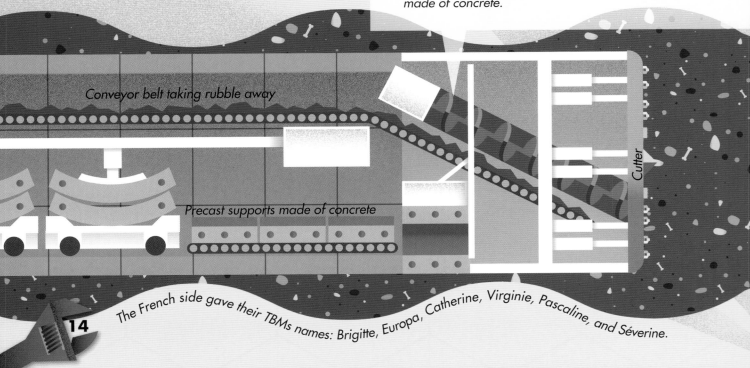

Conveyor belt taking rubble away

Precast supports made of concrete

Cutter

The French side gave their TBMs names: Brigitte, Europa, Catherine, Virginie, Pascaline, and Séverine.

TUNNEL GEOGRAPHY

The Channel Tunnel is actually three tunnels. Two larger outside tunnels carry the trains in each direction. A service tunnel in the middle is used for repairs or emergency vehicles. They are linked every 1,230 ft to allow for an escape route in an emergency. There are also two enormous **caverns** along the route that allow trains to cross from one line to the other if there is a problem. Each tunnel can be closed off from the other to shut out smoke if there is a fire. A **piston relief duct** connects the two rail tunnels at the top. This duct allows air to be pushed between the two tunnels as the trains fly by and alter the air pressure.

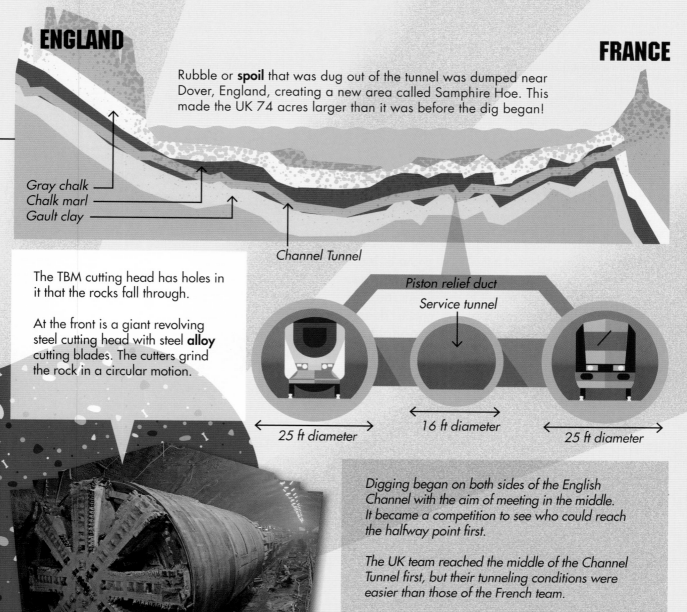

ENGLAND

FRANCE

Rubble or **spoil** that was dug out of the tunnel was dumped near Dover, England, creating a new area called Samphire Hoe. This made the UK 74 acres larger than it was before the dig began!

Gray chalk
Chalk marl
Gault clay

Channel Tunnel

The TBM cutting head has holes in it that the rocks fall through.

At the front is a giant revolving steel cutting head with steel **alloy** cutting blades. The cutters grind the rock in a circular motion.

Piston relief duct
Service tunnel

25 ft diameter   16 ft diameter   25 ft diameter

Digging began on both sides of the English Channel with the aim of meeting in the middle. It became a competition to see who could reach the halfway point first.

The UK team reached the middle of the Channel Tunnel first, but their tunneling conditions were easier than those of the French team.

DROGDEN TUNNEL

Did you know that Sweden and Denmark are connected by a bridge that turns into a tunnel? The dazzling engineering combination of the Øresund Bridge and the Drogden Tunnel also includes the artificial island of Perberholm. Together, the three projects form one of the most impressive engineering projects in the world.

Øresund Bridge

BUILDING BRIEF

Design a link to reach across the 10 mi stretch of water between the Swedish city of Malmö and the Danish capital, Copenhagen, to improve trade and tourism. The link must not disrupt shipping in the area or aircraft approaching Copenhagen Airport and must have minimal environmental impact.

Bridge architect: George K.S. Rotne

Tunnel design and construction: Arup

Location: Malmö, Sweden and Copenhagen, Denmark

THE TUNNEL

It was impossible to dig into the rock under the Drogden Channel, so engineers came up with a plan to rest the tunnel on the seabed. A narrow channel was dug with **dredging** diggers loading the spoil material onto barges to be taken away.

Precast concrete sections of the tunnel were manufactured on shore, sealed to make them watertight, and floated out into position. Once above their final positions, they were sunk carefully to rest in the trench on the seabed. The tunnel sections were then buried to stop them from floating away when the water was pumped out. Once buried, the water was pumped out so the tunnel lining could be completed.

THE BRIDGE

The Øresund Bridge is nearly 5 mi long and stands 187 ft above the water. This height allows tall ships to pass under the bridge. The bridge opened in July 2000 and is the longest combination rail and road bridge in Europe. The railway runs on a lower deck and vehicle traffic runs on the upper deck.

THE ISLAND

Dredged material from digging the tunnel was used to build up an area in the middle of the channel, which is now the island of Perberholm. This island is where the bridge ends and the tunnel begins. From that point on, the road and railway run alongside each other.

The island of Perberholm is protected in order to attract plants, animals, and birds. It is now home to more than 500 different species of plants.

The tunnel has five sections — two for cars, two for trains, and one section used for cables, servicing the tunnel, and an escape route.

The tunnel is 2.5 mi long and connects to the Danish island of Amager, a suburb of Copenhagen.

Service and escape tunnel

Cable duct

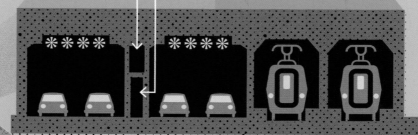

LÆRDAL TUNNEL

At 15.2 mi, the Lærdal Tunnel in Norway is the longest road tunnel in the world. It opened in November 2000 and provides a link between two of Norway's major cities. Directing a route underground avoided difficult terrain and left the beautiful Norwegian countryside undisturbed.

BUILDING BRIEF

Design a tunnel to connect the Norwegian cities of Oslo and Bergen, and provide a reliable link across the mountainous region and the many **fjords**.

Operator: Norwegian Public Roads Administration

Location: Lærdal and Aurland, Norway

DRILLING AND BLASTING

A moveable drilling jumbo machine was used to dig the tunnel by drilling and blasting. It drilled holes into the rock face that were then filled with explosives to blast the rock away.

A computer worked out the locations to drill and blast, and the positions were marked on the rock face with a **laser beam**. It took 5,000 blasts to clear the whole tunnel. That's 5.5 million pounds of explosives!

SCALING AND BOLTING

Creating a tunnel is dangerous work. Blasting and removing material can weaken the rock left behind. The force of the rock above needs to settle and redirect its weight around the new tunnel. This can put so much pressure on areas of weak rock that they explode. This is called a rock burst.

To stop rock bursts inside the Lærdal Tunnel, it was reinforced using a process called scaling and bolting. Steel bolts were shot into the newly exposed surface, redirecting any weaknesses deeper into the rock. The whole area was then sprayed with shotcrete, a quick-drying liquid concrete reinforced with plastic fibers. It took about 200,000 rock bolts and nearly 12 million gallons of shotcrete to secure the tunnel.

Steel bolts in the rock face

Spraying shotcrete

Drilling jumbo machine

LIGHT SHOW

To keep motorists awake and alert while driving the 20-minute journey underground, the engineers consulted with **psychologists** and came up with some neat tricks to stop any boredom. Fresh air is provided through the tunnel with fans placed at either end with an air filtration area in the middle. There are three caves along the drive that open out into areas big enough and safe enough to turn around in and to give the driver a break from the white light of the tunnel. The caves are illuminated with blue light, while yellow lights at the edges are designed to look like a sunrise.

BOSTON BIG DIG

By the 1980s, the roads of Boston, Massachusetts, were no longer able to cope with the city's increased traffic. The solution was the Big Dig, an enormous engineering feat that took 16 years to build. The Big Dig created tunnels that put some main city roads underground. Another tunnel was built under Boston Harbor.

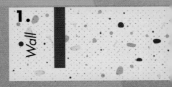

- — Existing road
- — New road
- — New tunnel

BUILDING BRIEF

Design and construct a new underground road system for the city of Boston. It should ease the increasing traffic and provide new links around the city.

Engineers: Bill Reynolds, Frederick P. Salvucci

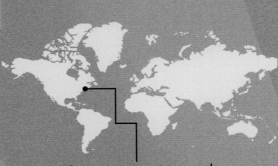

Location: Boston, Massachusetts

SLURRY WALLS

Slurry walls made it possible for engineers to tunnel through Boston's soft, watery soil. To build a slurry wall:

1. a guide wall is built and a trench is dug alongside it;

2. as the wall is built, it is filled with slurry. The pressure of the slurry prevents the walls of the trench from collapsing;

3. a steel cage is put into the slurry. Concrete is then pumped into the trench, starting at the bottom. As the concrete is pumped in, it pushes the slurry out. Once set, the concrete forms a single panel to the tunnel wall.

1. Wall

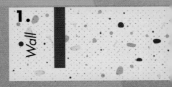
2. Slurry

3. Cage

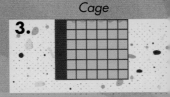

GROUND FREEZING

Ground-freezing pipe

Some of the ground around Boston is very soft and difficult to **excavate**, so engineers froze the ground temporarily to stabilize it as they dug. To do this, special pipes were put into the ground and cooled with salt water or **liquid nitrogen**, turning the water in the surrounding soil to ice.

BOSTON

Subway

Transitway

Central artery
roadway

Boston road and tunnel map

The Boston Big Dig created lots of different
tunnels under the city to accommodate
pedestrains, trains, buses, and cars.

TUNNEL JACKING

Tunnels had to be built under rail lines that were in
constant use. To do this, engineers needed to use
a technique called tunnel jacking. This involved
pushing a huge, hollow concrete box through the
earth, in this case directly under the rail lines. As
it is pushed through the earth, the dirt was dug
out and removed from the box. As the box moved
forward, supports were added to the empty tunnel
space behind it.

Push

TED WILLIAMS TUNNEL

The Ted Williams Tunnel was built under
Boston Harbor as an extra highway. It
is 1.6 mi long and was made from steel
sections covered in concrete. The twin-
tubed sections, which resemble giant
binoculars, were made off-site and floated
into place. They were laid in a dredged
channel and joined together to form the
tunnel. Each tube carries two lanes of
traffic. The tunnel is named after a famous
Boston Red Sox baseball player and was
opened to all traffic in 2003.

SMART TUNNEL

The SMART Tunnel, in Kuala Lumpur, Malaysia, stands for Stormwater Management and Road Tunnel—and it is a very smart tunnel indeed! It helps with the heavy traffic in the area and also provides a fantastic drainage system in times of flooding. The SMART Tunnel opened in 2007.

BUILDING BRIEF

Design and build a tunnel to carry floodwater from the Klang and Gombak rivers away from the center of the city and add sections for cars.

Engineer: MMC Engineering-Gamuda, Mott MacDonald and SSP Consultants, Gustav Klados (Senior Project Manager)

Location: Kuala Lumpur, Malaysia

DUAL PURPOSE

When designing the stormwater tunnel, engineers decided that it could also be used as a road link. Cars could then travel under the city rather than through it. So the tunnel was built with two road sections and a section at the bottom for floodwater.

Semitrucks and motorbikes are not allowed to use the tunnel because they may cause more accidents than cars alone.

The tunnel is 6 mi long, of which 2.5 mi is used as a roadway for cars. It is 43 ft in diameter.

CRACKS AND CAVES

The tunnel was dug with two specially designed TBMs. They started in the middle of the tunnel and dug outward. The ground in Kuala Lumpur sits on **limestone**, which can be dotted with caves and caverns.

Geologists bored holes ahead of the TBMs to check for breaks in the stone structure. If a TBM dug into a space under the ground, it could open up a great cavern called a **sinkhole**. Where cracks, holes, and other weaknesses were discovered, a concrete-based grout was pumped in to fill the empty spaces. This provided a soft and safe ground for the TBM to drill into.

THREE MODES

The completed tunnel operates in three modes:

Mode 1—*When there is little or no rain, the cars can use the two road tiers of the tunnel.*

Mode 2—*When there is moderate rain, cars can use the two tiers of road, but the bottom drainage tier is also used to direct rainwater to a river south of the city.*

Mode 3—*About twice a year when there is heavy rain and the city is in danger of flooding, the tunnel is closed to cars and the stormwater is allowed to flow through all three sections of the tunnel.*

After the tunnel has been used for floodwater, it is cleaned before cars are allowed to use it again. This takes about two days.

LARGE HADRON COLLIDER

The Large Hadron Collider Tunnel is different from other tunnels in many ways. It's not a transport link. It doesn't channel water. And it's completely circular! The tunnel has a circumference of nearly 17 mi and is home to the Large Hadron Collider—an instrument that tries to reproduce the conditions that existed at the time of the Big Bang.

BUILDING BRIEF

Use an existing tunnel to house the Large Hadron Collider.

Construction project engineer: John Osborne at CERN

Location: Geneva, Switzerland

The Large Hadron Collider was built by CERN—the European Council for Nuclear Research—an organization that was founded in 1954.

THE TUNNEL

The tunnel was excavated between 1985 and 1988 using three TBMs. It was originally designed for an earlier machine—the Large Electron–Positron Collider. In places, the tunnel is nearly 330 ft underground. Experiments are easier to control there because they are unaffected by temperature change and **radiation** from the sun. The Large Hadron Collider's first experiment took place in 2008.

WHAT THE LARGE HADRON COLLIDER DOES

The Large Hadron Collider is the largest and most powerful particle accelerator in the world. A particle accelerator is a machine that sends two particle beams in opposite directions around the tunnel at almost the speed of light, in the hope that they will collide. Magnets placed around the tunnel make the beams curve. Meanwhile, four particle detectors gather clues about the collision of particles, to help scientists understand more about the beginning of the universe.

FRANCE

Large →
Hadron
Collider

CERN
laboratory

SWITZERLAND

The tunnel crosses the border between France and Switzerland.

A particle detector

MOON MOVEMENT

Although placing the Hadron Collider underground means that conditions for experiments are easier to control, there is one day of the month when things change. On nights when there is a full moon, Earth's crust rises by about 10 inches. This causes the tunnel edge, or circumference, to stretch by about 1 millimeter. This is not a huge change, but it's big enough that scientists have to take it into account as they study their test results.

What is **dark matter**? What are **black holes**? Scientists at CERN hope that the Large Hadron Collider will help them discover the answers to these big questions and many more.

GOTTHARD BASE TUNNEL

Many tunnels run beneath the mountains of the Alps, but the longest and deepest of them all is the Gotthard Base Tunnel, which was completed in 2016.

BUILDING BRIEF

Design a rail link through the Saint-Gotthard Massif mountain range to provide high-speed rail links through Switzerland.

Engineers: Ernst Basler + Partner, AlpTransit

Location: Switzerland

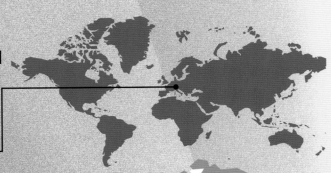

Switzerland

Tunnel route →

DESIGN AND ROUTE

Extensive geological testing had to be carried out to make sure that the mountain rock was stable enough for drilling and could support a tunnel. During the testing, a hole was drilled through an area of rock that had water behind it. This caused the test tunnel to fill with high-pressure water, so the tunnel was redirected to find a deeper route.

Tests showed that the rock much lower down was marble—a hard rock perfect for tunneling. As a result, it is the deepest rail tunnel in the world, reaching 1.4 mi under the ground in some parts.

At 35 mi long, the Gotthard Base Tunnel is the longest rail tunnel in the world.

PLAN OF WORKS

To complete the massive dig in time, tunneling started in four different places along the route— in Erstfeld, Amsteg, Sedrun, and Faido. A station in Bodio, at the end of the tunnel, was added later. The project used four gigantic TBMs that could tunnel nearly 7 ft at a time. The TBMs dug through the rock and sprayed the uncovered surface with liquid concrete to stabilize the newly dug areas. Work went on for 24 hours a day for six years. There were up to 1,000 people working in the tunnel at a time.

INNER WATERPROOFING

The inner surface of the tunnel was made from concrete. Liquid concrete was added at the first stage to temporarily support the tunnel roof. In some areas where there was groundwater, extra material layers were added for waterproofing. First, a layer of plastic mesh was added, then a layer of plastic sheeting. This keeps the groundwater from running around the tunnel. A metal mold was then pulled through and normal concrete was poured behind to complete the tunnel lining.

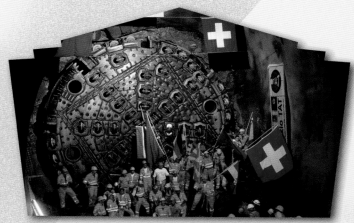

Workers celebrate after the TBM breaks through the rock, completing the tunnel.

Plastic sheeting
Plastic mesh
Concrete
Metal mold

A worker sprays concrete onto the walls of the Sedrun section of the tunnel.

FASCINATING FACTS

Many tunnels run under the ground. There might even be a tunnel under your feet right now!

The Marmaray Tunnel, which opened in 2013, is a tube sunk under the Bosphorus Strait in Istanbul, Turkey. The Bosphorus Strait splits the city, so one side is in Europe and the other side is in Asia. The tunnel links these two continents, so by train it takes just four minutes to get from Europe to Asia.

In Shanghai, China, the Bund Sightseeing Tunnel takes visitors on a short, colorful 2,123 ft trip by train through a tunnel of bright lights, sound effects, and music.

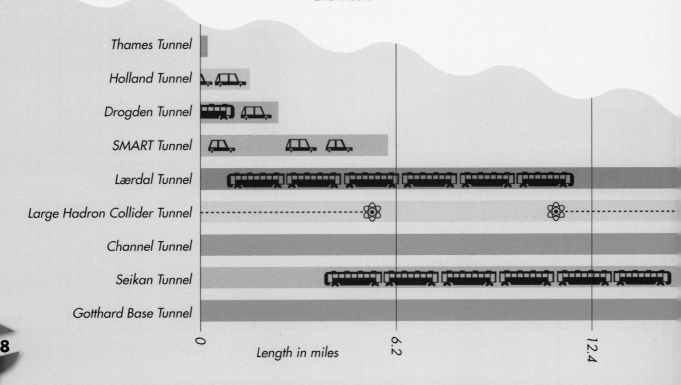

Thames Tunnel
Holland Tunnel
Drogden Tunnel
SMART Tunnel
Lærdal Tunnel
Large Hadron Collider Tunnel
Channel Tunnel
Seikan Tunnel
Gotthard Base Tunnel

0   6.2   12.4

Length in miles

The world's longest waterslide tunnel is the Magic Eye at Galaxy Erding Waterpark in Germany. It's a nearly 1,200 ft long ride in a giant rubber raft.

The largest wind tunnel in the world is at the NASA Ames Research Center in Mountain View, California. It is nearly 1,400 ft long and 180 ft high. It has two test areas and is big enough to house a full-size plane. In this photo, a parachute designed for a mission to Mars is being tested.

The Lincoln Tunnel links Weehawken, New Jersey and Midtown Manhattan in New York City. It's used by 120,000 vehicles every day, making it one of the world's busiest tunnels.

Chiang Mai Zoo Aquarium in Thailand has the longest aqua tunnel in the world. Visitors can walk through the tunnel—which is 436 ft long—and see up to 250 different species of fish and aquatic animals through the glass.

18.6

24.8

31

37.2

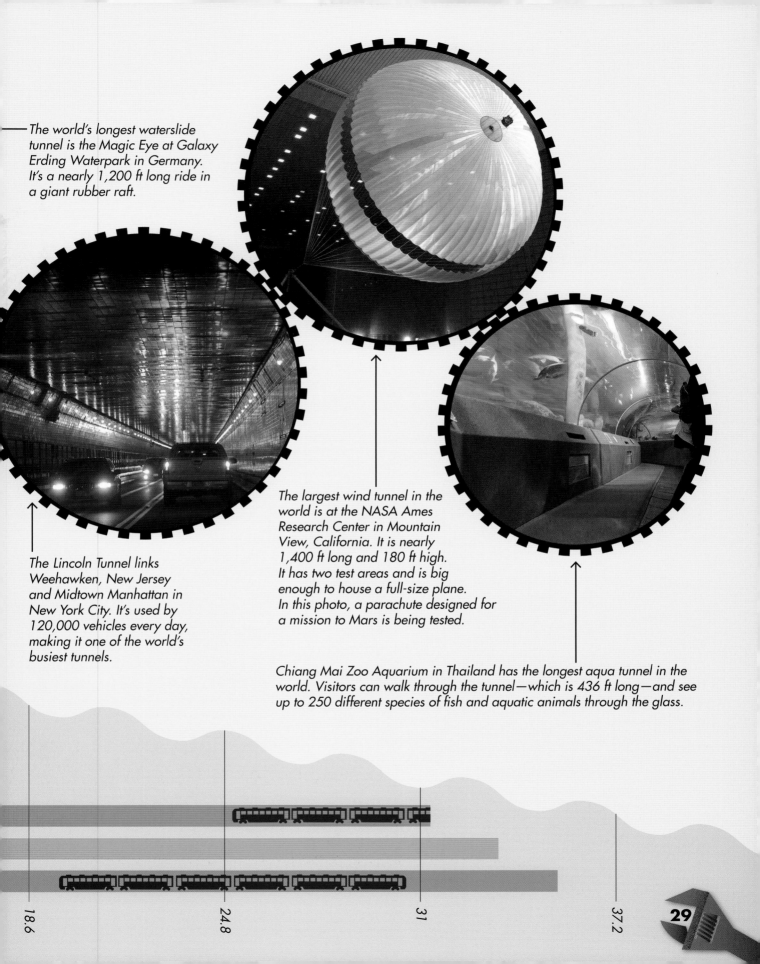

READ MORE

Bell, Samantha S. *Building Tunnels.* Engineering Challenges. Mendota Heights, Minn.: North Star Editions, 2017.

Hardyman, Robyn. *Tunnels.* Engineering Eurekas. New York: PowerKids Press, 2017.

Mattern, Joanne. *Tunnels.* Engineering Wonders. Vero Beach, Fla.: Rourke Educational Media, 2015.

Sikkens, Crystal. *A Tunnel Runs Through.* Be an Engineer! Designing to Solve Problems. New York: Crabtree Publishing Company, 2017.

INTERNET SITES

FactHound offers a safe, fun way to find Internet sites related to this book. All of the sites on FactHound have been researched by our staff.

Here's all you do:

Visit www.facthound.com

Type in this code: 9781543513387

Check out projects, games and lots more at
www.capstonekids.com

GLOSSARY

alloy a substance made by melting and mixing two or more metals with another substance

black hole an area of space with such a strong gravitational field that not even light can escape from it

bore to make a hole in something with a drill or similar tool

caisson a tube or box in which people and machines can work under water; caissons are later filled with concrete and used to support bridges and buildings

cast iron a hard and brittle form of iron made by melting iron with carbon, and silicon

cavern a deep hollow place underground

ceramic an object made out of clay

compressed air air that has been put under greater pressure than the air around us

concrete a building material made from a mixture of sand, gravel, cement, and water

conveyor belt a moving belt that carries objects from one place to another

dark matter invisible energy and matter that scientists can't detect but believe is out in space

dredge to scrape the bottom of a body of water to make it deeper

engineering to process of designing and building machines, vehicles, bridges, roads, or other structures

excavate to dig in the earth

fjord a long, narrow inlet of ocean between high cliffs

foundation a solid structure on which a building is built

geologist a scientist who studies how Earth formed and how it changes by examining soil, rocks, rivers, and other landforms

gravity a force that pulls objects with mass together; gravity pulls objects down toward the center of Earth

grout a thin paste or material used for filling gaps between bricks, slabs, and tiles.

innovative advanced or unlike anything done before

iron a strong, hard metal used in buildings

landscape the natural state or landforms of an area

laser beam a thin, intense, high-energy ray of light

limestone a hard white or gray stone, often used as a building material

liquid nitrogen a liquid formed after nitrogen gas is pressurized and cooled

piston relief duct in the Channel Tunnel, an air duct that links the two rail tunnels and helps to limit the changes in air pressure as trains pass by

precast a concrete object that has been molded (cast) into shape before being placed in its final position

psychologist a person who studies people's minds, emotions, and the ways they behave

radiation energy waves

sewer a system of underground pipes that carry away liquid and solid waste

shotcrete a mixture of cement, sand and water

sinkhole a hollow place in the ground where drainage collects

spoil rubble or waste material removed when digging in the earth

stabilize to make or become stable, fixed, or steady

steel a strong, hard metal formed from iron, carbon, and other materials

terrain the surface of the land

trench a long, narrow ditch dug in the ground

ventilation a system that allows the flow of fresh air

INDEX